Urban Exploration - New York The Comprehensive Travel Guide

PA BOOKS

Published by PA BOOKS, 2023.

URBAN EXPLORATION - NEW YORK THE COMPREHENSIVE TRAVEL GUIDE

First edition. October 28, 2023.

Copyright © 2023 PA BOOKS.

ISBN: 979-8223215400

Written by PA BOOKS.

Also by PA BOOKS

Hogan's Key
Kimberly & the Five Strange Goldfishes
The Enchanted Library
The Misadventures of Pirate Pete
From Wheel To Web: 40 Remarkable Inventions
Once Upon A Sleepy Time
The Global Game - The Evolution Of Football
Strides To Success: A Beginner's Guide to Running
The ChatGPT Handbook
Climate Crossroads
1000 Everyday Life Hacks
Urban Exploration - London The Comprehensive Travel Guide
Urban Exploration - New York The Comprehensive Travel Guide
Urban Exploration - Amsterdam The Comprehensive Travel Guide
Urban Exploration - Barcelona The Comprehensive Travel Guide
Urban Exploration - Dubai The Comprehensive Travel Guide
Urban Exploration - Paris The Comprehensive Travel Guide

Table of Contents

Chapter 1: Introduction to New York City

The New York Experience

Welcome to New York City, a vibrant, multifaceted metropolis that beckons explorers, dreamers, and wanderers from around the world. In this chapter, we'll embark on a journey to discover the heart of this magnificent city, from its storied past to the unique experiences that make it an urban explorer's paradise.

Unveiling the City

New York City, often lovingly called the "Big Apple," is a place where the past meets the present, and cultures from every corner of the globe harmoniously blend. This sprawling metropolis, nestled in the south-eastern corner of New York State, stands as the most populous city in the United States. Its five boroughs—Manhattan, Brooklyn, Queens, The Bronx, and Staten Island—encompass a wide array of neighbourhoods, each with its own character and charm.

A Glimpse into History

To truly appreciate New York City, it's essential to understand its rich history. The city's roots can be traced back to 1624 when the Dutch West India Company established New Amsterdam, a trading post at the southern tip of Manhattan. In 1664, the English seized control, renaming it New York. Over centuries, waves of immigrants brought their traditions, languages, and dreams to this thriving melting pot, contributing to the city's extraordinary diversity and cultural vibrancy.

The Unique Allure of New York

What sets New York City apart is its incomparable blend of old-world charm and cutting-edge innovation. It is home to the world's most iconic skyscrapers, renowned museums, world-class theatres, and bustling neighbourhoods, all infused with an electrifying energy that is uniquely New York. Here, tradition and modernity coexist, creating an urban landscape that invites exploration and invites the curious to unearth hidden treasures.

Navigating the Labyrinth

Getting Around the City

Navigating New York City is a fundamental aspect of your adventure. Luckily, this metropolis boasts a comprehensive public transportation system that can swiftly transport you to your desired destinations. The New York City Subway, the largest in the world, spans the city with its 24 subway lines, ensuring you are well-connected to virtually every corner. Acquiring a Metro Card will provide access to subways and buses, making travel in the city both convenient and economical.

Your Home in the City

Choosing the right accommodation is pivotal to a memorable journey. New York City offers a diverse array of lodging options, catering to every budget and taste. From luxury hotels that offer breath-taking skyline views to charming bed-and-breakfasts nestled in historic neighbourhoods, you are sure to discover the perfect place to call home during your visit. Reserving your accommodation well in advance is advisable, as New York is a year-round tourist magnet.

Prioritizing Safety

While New York City is generally a safe destination for tourists, it is imperative to prioritize personal safety. Keep your belongings secure, stay vigilant in unfamiliar areas, and avoid poorly lit or isolated spots, particularly after dark. The city's police force is dedicated to maintaining a safe environment for both residents and visitors, but vigilance is key.

Experiencing the Seasons

New York City experiences distinct seasons, each presenting a unique perspective of the city. Spring offers blooming cherry blossoms and outdoor events, while summer invites exploration of parks and beaches. Fall blankets the city in vivid foliage, and winter transforms it into a magical wonderland with holiday decorations and ice skating rinks.

Neighbourhood Gems

Let's delve deeper into the five boroughs and the distinct neighbourhoods that constitute the vibrant tapestry of New York City.

Manhattan: The Epicentre of Excitement

Manhattan stands as the epicentre of the city's activity, boasting iconic neighbourhoods like Midtown, the Upper West Side, and the East Village. The borough is synonymous with towering skyscrapers, renowned museums, and the perennially vibrant Times Square. Explore the historical charm of Greenwich Village, where the Beat Generation thrived, or the luxury boutiques of Soho.

Brooklyn: A Hub of Creativity

Just across the East River from Manhattan lies Brooklyn, a borough synonymous with creativity and innovation. Williamsburg is an artistic hub, while DUMBO enchants with cobblestone streets and breath-taking views of the Manhattan skyline. Don't forget to visit Coney Island for a taste of classic amusements and a stroll along the iconic boardwalk.

Queens: The Global Melting Pot

Queens, known as "The World's Borough," offers a mosaic of cultures from across the globe. Flushing is a food lover's paradise, offering delectable international cuisine, while Astoria is celebrated for its Greek culture and vibrant nightlife. Jackson Heights embodies multicultural diversity, and Long Island City hosts art galleries and scenic waterfront parks.

The Bronx: A Cultural Hub

The Bronx has a rich cultural history, often associated with the birth of hip-hop and the legendary Yankee Stadium. Explore the Bronx Museum of the Arts, wander through the New York Botanical Garden, or uncover hidden gems in historic neighbourhoods like Mott Haven and Belmont.

Staten Island: A Tranquil Escape

A short ferry ride from Manhattan, Staten Island often remains undiscovered by tourists, but it possesses its own unique charm. Explore the expansive Staten Island Greenbelt, an urban oasis, or visit the Staten Island Museum to uncover the borough's rich history. The Staten Island

Ferry provides an iconic, free journey with breath-taking views of the Statue of Liberty and Lower Manhattan.

Conclusion

New York City is a city of dreams, a place where countless stories have unfurled and adventures have taken flight. This guidebook will be your compass as we uncover the hidden gems, delve into the local culture, and explore the unique neighbourhoods that define the enigmatic personality of New York City. As you embark on your urban exploration journey, be prepared to be entranced by the pulsating energy, diversity, and awe that New York City embodies. From the historical avenues of Manhattan to the artistic enclaves of Brooklyn and the cultural quilt of Queens, each corner of this city has a story waiting to be unearthed, waiting for you to discover.

Chapter 2: Exploring Brooklyn's Vibrant Neighbourhoods

Brooklyn's Distinctive Charm

Brooklyn, one of New York City's five boroughs, is a world unto itself. It's a place where historic neighbourhoods seamlessly blend with contemporary art, artisanal dining, and a rich cultural tapestry. In this chapter, we invite you to immerse yourself in the heart of Brooklyn and explore its diverse neighbourhoods, each with a unique character and charm.

Williamsburg: The Epicentre of Cool

Williamsburg, often hailed as the hipster capital of the world, is a neighbourhood that teems with creativity, culture, and innovation. Walk down its streets, and you'll encounter a vibrant arts scene, trendy boutiques, and a dynamic dining culture.

Local Art Scene

Williamsburg's creative spirit is evident around every corner. The neighbourhood houses numerous art galleries, like the Williamsburg Art & Historical Centre, featuring local and international talent. Stroll down Bedford Avenue, which is known for its street art, and you'll witness an ever-evolving outdoor gallery of murals and graffiti that reflects the neighbourhood's artistic flair.

Street Art

As you explore Williamsburg's streets, you'll be struck by the abundance of street art. The neighbourhood has embraced urban art with gusto. Look out for the towering murals and intricate stencils that adorn buildings, making the streets a living canvas of artistic expression.

Cultural Attractions

Williamsburg isn't all about art; it also has cultural gems. The Brooklyn Brewery, a beloved institution, offers tours and tastings of its craft beers. The Music Hall of Williamsburg hosts concerts from a wide range of musical genres, from indie rock to electronic. For something more unconventional, the City Reliquary Museum showcases a collection of quirky New York artefacts.

Hidden Culinary Gems

Williamsburg's dining scene is a kaleidoscope of flavours. Be sure to visit Smorgasburg, a food market that brings together an array of gourmet vendors. Don't miss out on the local favourite, Peter Luger Steak House, a legendary eatery that's been serving up mouth-watering steaks since 1887. Additionally, Williamsburg's food truck scene is a treasure trove of delectable bites, often parked near the waterfront.

DUMBO: Cobblestones and Creativity

DUMBO, short for Down Under the Manhattan Bridge Overpass, is a neighbourhood with a distinct blend of history and innovation. Nestled between the Brooklyn and Manhattan Bridges, DUMBO is famous for its cobblestone streets, stunning views, and a thriving arts community.

Local Art Scene

DUMBO's art scene is deeply ingrained in its industrial past. The neighbourhood is home to numerous galleries, such as the A.I.R. Gallery, which exclusively features female artists. Be sure to visit Smack Mellon, a non-profit gallery known for its cutting-edge exhibitions.

Street Art

The streets of DUMBO are adorned with art installations and sculptures, contributing to its reputation as an open-air gallery. Stroll along Washington Street for the iconic view framed by the Manhattan Bridge, offering one of the most photographed scenes in New York.

Cultural Attractions

DUMBO is not just about visuals; it's also home to the renowned St. Ann's Warehouse, an avant-garde theatre space hosting experimental performances and productions. Additionally, you can visit the impressive Jacques Torres Chocolate Factory for a behind-the-scenes look at the chocolate-making process.

Hidden Culinary Gems

DUMBO offers a culinary journey that is nothing short of delightful. The River Café, located on the waterfront, provides a romantic setting and exceptional French-American cuisine. For a more casual experience, head to the Brooklyn Ice Cream Factory for classic ice cream with unparalleled views of the city.

Red Hook: Quaint and Industrial

Red Hook is a neighbourhood with a character all its own. It's an industrial area that has undergone a transformation into a hub of creativity and local culture.

Local Art Scene

Red Hook's art scene is best experienced at Pioneer Works, a cultural centre dedicated to art, science, and innovation. It hosts exhibitions, performances, and lectures that foster creative expression.

Street Art

While Red Hook may not be as renowned for street art as Williamsburg or DUMBO, its industrial backdrop provides a unique canvas for graffiti artists. Look out for the art that adorns warehouses and the backstreets.

Cultural Attractions

The Red Hook waterfront is home to the Red Hook Waterfront Museum, housed in a beautifully restored 1914 barge. It offers a glimpse into the maritime history of the area. Additionally, IKEA enthusiasts might want to visit the local store, known for its scenic views and Swedish delicacies.

Hidden Culinary Gems

Red Hook offers a range of culinary experiences. The Red Hook Lobster Pound is a must-visit for seafood enthusiasts, serving up some of the freshest lobster rolls in the city. For a unique experience, explore the food vendors at Red Hook Ball Fields, where you can savour delicious Latin American street food.

Partaking in Brooklyn's Culinary Scene

Brooklyn is a culinary wonderland with a dizzying array of dining options. While we've highlighted hidden gems in each neighbourhood, don't forget to explore Brooklyn's thriving food culture more extensively. From artisanal bakeries to global cuisine, you'll find something to satisfy every palate. And be sure to try Brooklyn's famous pizza, rivalling that of any other city.

Brooklyn's Cafe Culture

Brooklyn's cafe culture is a testament to the borough's creativity and individuality. The coffee shops here offer more than just a caffeine fix; they provide a glimpse into the local lifestyle. Be it a cosy corner in a bookshop cafe or a trendy spot for latte art, Brooklyn's cafes welcome explorers seeking respite and inspiration.

Conclusion

Brooklyn is a haven for those who yearn to explore unique neighbourhoods where creativity thrives, street art tells stories, and diverse culinary adventures await. From the trendy streets of Williamsburg to the cobblestone pathways of DUMBO and the industrial charm of Red Hook, Brooklyn is a dynamic tapestry of local culture and innovation. Each neighbourhood has its distinctive character, offering a trove of hidden gems waiting to be discovered by urban explorers.

Chapter 3: Unearthing History in Lower Manhattan

Lower Manhattan's Rich Tapestry

Lower Manhattan, a storied district at the southern tip of the island of Manhattan, stands as the historical nucleus of New York City. This iconic part of the city has borne witness to countless pivotal events, from the founding of New Amsterdam to the horrors of 9/11. In this chapter, we will guide you through the historical significance of Lower Manhattan, uncovering its hidden gems, and sharing lesser-known stories that lie beneath the surface.

Financial District: The Heart of Commerce

Lower Manhattan's Financial District is a global symbol of economic power and is home to iconic landmarks such as Wall Street and the New York Stock Exchange. It's a district that boasts more than just financial institutions; it's an area where history, architecture, and culture converge.

Historical Significance

Begin your exploration in the heart of Lower Manhattan at Federal Hall, the site where George Washington was inaugurated as the first President of the United States. The building also served as the nation's first capitol. Nearby stands the Charging Bull, a symbol of Wall Street's financial optimism, and the Fearless Girl statue, representing female empowerment in the world of finance.

Hidden Historical Sites

Discover the Fraunces Tavern Museum, a historical treasure that was once a tavern and a meeting place for George Washington and his officers during the American Revolution. Immerse yourself in the rich history of the district at the Museum of American Finance, which features exhibits on the financial markets and their impact on American life.

Lesser-Known Stories

Few visitors are aware of the India House, an elegant, private club dating back to 1851, which once counted Mark Twain and Nikola Tesla as members. Learn about the Trial of the Century at 65 Broad Street, where the infamous Charles Ponzi was put on trial for his eponymous scheme.

South Street Seaport: A Maritime Legacy

South Street Seaport, often referred to as the "Museum of the City's Future," is a preserved 19th-century port with historic ships, cobblestone streets, and a maritime museum. It's a journey back in time, and the stories of the district are steeped in the salt and brine of the sea.

Historical Significance

As you stroll along the waterfront, the South Street Seaport Museum is a must-visit, offering insight into the area's maritime heritage. Explore tall ships like the Wavertree and Peking, both of which provide a tangible link to the seafaring past of New York City.

Hidden Historical Sites

Visit the Titanic Memorial Lighthouse, a poignant monument to the tragic sinking of the Titanic in 1912. Nearby, at the Ambrose Lightship Museum, you can step aboard a floating lighthouse that once guided ships into New York Harbour.

Lesser-Known Stories

The haunting tale of the Tugboat and the Lighthouse tells of a collision between a tugboat and a lighthouse in 1951, leading to the tragic loss of several lives. This lesser-known event is commemorated in a plaque on the waterfront.

9/11 Memorial: Honouring the Fallen

The 9/11 Memorial, located at the World Trade Centre site, is a sombre but essential visit. This solemn memorial pays tribute to the nearly 3,000 victims of the terrorist attacks on September 11, 2001. It's a place for reflection, remembrance, and resilience.

Historical Significance

The 9/11 Memorial is centred around two enormous reflecting pools set within the footprints of the Twin Towers. The pools are surrounded by bronze parapets inscribed with the names of the victims, offering a poignant reminder of the tragedy.

Hidden Historical Sites

While the 9/11 Memorial is widely known, few visitors realize that the Survivor Tree, a Callery pear tree recovered from the rubble of the Twin

Towers, was nursed back to health and now stands as a symbol of hope. Nearby, the FDNY Memorial Wall honours fire-fighters who died on 9/11.

Lesser-Known Stories

The 9/11 Memorial Museum contains countless stories of heroism and loss, including the accounts of the first responders who rushed into the buildings. This museum provides a comprehensive look at the events of that fateful day.

A Walk through Time

Lower Manhattan is a district that bridges the past and present. From the cobblestone streets of South Street Seaport to the solemn waters of the 9/11 Memorial, the district is a living testament to the history of New York City. As you explore these significant sites, you'll uncover stories of resilience, triumph, and courage that have shaped the city.

Guided Tours

Consider taking a guided walking tour of Lower Manhattan to gain a deeper understanding of its history. Knowledgeable guides will provide you with unique insights into the district's lesser-known stories, hidden historical sites, and the events that have defined this iconic part of the city.

Conclusion

Lower Manhattan is a district where history echoes through the streets, and the legacy of the past is ever-present. From the powerful symbolism of the Financial District to the maritime heritage of South Street Seaport and the solemnity of the 9/11 Memorial, this part of New York City tells a story of resilience and remembrance. As you explore Lower Manhattan, you'll find that it's a journey through time, where the past informs the present, and where stories of triumph and tragedy merge to create an indelible historical tapestry.

Chapter 4: Harlem's Cultural Renaissance

Harlem: A Cultural Tapestry

Harlem, a neighbourhood located in the northern part of Manhattan, is a legendary hub of artistic expression and cultural heritage. With a history steeped in the African American experience, Harlem has become synonymous with jazz, soul food, dance, and a rich historical narrative. In this chapter, we will delve into Harlem's vibrant cultural scene, showcasing its musical legacy, dance traditions, and the institutions that have made it a symbol of cultural renewal.

Harlem's Musical Legacy

Harlem is world-renowned for its contributions to music, particularly in the realms of jazz and gospel. Its streets have echoed with the rhythms and melodies of musical legends, and this rich legacy continues to thrive.

Jazz Clubs

Harlem is a jazz lover's paradise, with numerous venues where you can immerse yourself in the genre's timeless rhythms. The legendary "Cotton Club" is a must-visit, known for hosting jazz luminaries like Duke Ellington and Cab Calloway in the past. The "Apollo Theatre" remains an iconic venue where music legends like Ella Fitzgerald and Billie Holiday once graced the stage. It hosts a range of musical genres, including jazz, R&B, and soul.

Gospel Music

For an authentic gospel experience, attend a Sunday morning church service in Harlem. The "Abyssinian Baptist Church" and "Canaan Baptist Church" are known for their inspiring gospel choirs and welcoming atmosphere. Visitors are often welcomed to join in the joyful celebration of music and faith.

Hidden Gems

Look out for smaller, more intimate jazz venues like "Minton's Playhouse", the birthplace of bebop, or "Silvana", a cosy spot known for its live jazz and multicultural cuisine. These venues offer a chance to connect with the soul of Harlem in a more personal setting.

Soul Food Dining

Harlem is a culinary mecca, celebrated for its soul food that reflects the deep-rooted history and culture of the African American community. These restaurants offer an authentic taste of the South in the heart of New York City.

Sylvia's Restaurant

No exploration of Harlem's soul food would be complete without a visit to "Sylvia's", often called the "Queen of Soul Food." Founded in 1962 by Sylvia Woods, the restaurant serves up delicious dishes like fried chicken, collard greens, and cornbread. It's a Harlem institution that has hosted celebrities and dignitaries from around the world.

Red Rooster Harlem

"Red Rooster Harlem", a vibrant eatery by renowned chef Marcus Samuelsson, offers a modern take on classic soul food dishes. The restaurant combines food, music, and art, creating an atmosphere that resonates with Harlem's cultural renaissance.

Morningside Park Farmers Market

For a taste of Harlem's fresh produce and homemade treats, visit the "Morningside Park Farmers Market", a weekly event featuring local vendors. You'll find everything from handcrafted pies to organic vegetables and artisanal cheeses.

The Apollo Theatre

The "Apollo Theatre" is an enduring symbol of Harlem's cultural significance. This historic venue has played a pivotal role in shaping the careers of countless musicians, dancers, and comedians. Opened in 1914, the Apollo has hosted legendary performers such as James Brown, Stevie Wonder, and Michael Jackson.

Amateur Night

Amateur Night at the Apollo is a storied tradition that dates back to the theatre's early years. It's a showcase for emerging talent and has served as a Launchpad for artists like Ella Fitzgerald and Jimi Hendrix. The audience's reaction is famously demanding, with the "Sandman" sweeping performers offstage if they don't meet the crowd's approval.

Apollo Theatre Tour

Take a tour of the Apollo Theatre to explore its rich history and get a behind-the-scenes look at the venue. You'll visit the dressing rooms, see the Wall of Fame, and learn about the artists who have made the Apollo a legendary cultural institution.

Events and Performances

Check the Apollo's calendar for upcoming events and performances, which range from music and comedy to dance and special presentations. Attending a show at the Apollo is a cultural experience like no other.

Harlem's Cultural Fusion

Harlem's cultural heritage is a fusion of African, Caribbean, and African American influences. The neighbourhood's diversity is evident in its art, music, and traditions, making it a dynamic and ever-evolving cultural tapestry.

Harlem Arts Scene

Harlem's artistic contributions extend beyond music, encompassing visual arts, dance, and theatre. The neighbourhood is home to a variety of cultural institutions and galleries that showcase both contemporary and historical works.

Studio Museum in Harlem

The "Studio Museum in Harlem" is a leading institution for contemporary art by African American artists. It features a diverse range of exhibitions, public programs, and educational initiatives that explore the connections between art and society.

Dance Theatre of Harlem

The "Dance Theatre of Harlem" is an iconic ballet company renowned for its ground-breaking performances. Founded in 1969 by Arthur Mitchell, the first African American principal dancer at the New York City Ballet, the company has broken barriers and transformed the world of dance.

National Jazz Museum in Harlem

For an in-depth exploration of the neighbourhood's jazz heritage, visit the "National Jazz Museum in Harlem". This institution hosts exhibitions, performances, and educational programs dedicated to preserving and promoting the art of jazz.

Schomburg Center for Research in Black Culture

The "Schomburg Center for Research in Black Culture", part of the New York Public Library, is a vital resource for African American history and culture. It houses a vast collection of books, photographs, manuscripts, and artefacts that shed light on the African diaspora and the black experience in America.

Conclusion

Harlem's cultural renaissance is a living testament to the neighbourhood's history, resilience, and creativity. Its iconic music venues, soul food restaurants, and artistic institutions serve as a reflection of its deep-rooted cultural legacy. As you explore Harlem's streets, you'll become a part of its ongoing cultural revival, where past, present, and future intersect.

In the chapters that follow, we'll continue to uncover the hidden gems, local culture, and unique experiences in New York City's diverse neighbourhoods.

Chapter 5: The Bronx: Beyond the Headlines

Uncovering the Real Bronx

The Bronx, often misunderstood and underestimated, is a borough teeming with culture, history, and diverse neighbourhoods. It's time to challenge the stereotypes and explore the unique attractions that make this part of New York City an unmissable destination. In this chapter, we'll venture into the Bronx's rich cultural institutions, vibrant parks, and the neighbourhoods that define its character.

The Bronx's Rich Cultural Institutions

The Bronx is home to a wealth of cultural institutions that celebrate art, history, and heritage. These institutions offer a window into the multifaceted nature of the borough.

The Bronx Museum of the Arts

"The Bronx Museum of the Arts" is a leading cultural institution dedicated to exhibiting works by artists of African, Asian, and Latin American descent. It's known for its contemporary art collections and community-based programs. The museum's diverse exhibitions highlight the Bronx's cultural vibrancy.

Bronx Music Heritage Center

The "Bronx Music Heritage Center" is a testament to the borough's significant role in the development of various musical genres. It's dedicated to preserving and celebrating the Bronx's musical heritage, from hip-hop to salsa. Visit this center to explore the borough's rich history of music.

Wave Hill

"Wave Hill" is a beautiful public garden and cultural center located in the Riverdale neighbourhood. It provides a tranquil escape from the hustle and bustle of the city and offers breath-taking views of the Hudson River and the Palisades. It hosts art exhibitions, workshops, and performances, making it a dynamic destination for nature and culture enthusiasts.

Bronx Parks: Green Oases

The Bronx boasts a stunning array of parks, making it a haven for nature lovers. These green spaces are a breath of fresh air in the urban landscape.

The New York Botanical Garden

"The New York Botanical Garden" is a living museum that showcases a breath-taking collection of plants from around the world. It's a place of natural beauty and serenity, with themed gardens, walking trails, and family-friendly exhibitions.

Bronx Zoo

The "Bronx Zoo" is one of the largest metropolitan zoos in the world. Its home to a wide range of animals and offers an educational and entertaining experience for visitors of all ages. The zoo's conservation efforts and immersive exhibits make it a must-visit destination.

Pelham Bay Park

"Pelham Bay Park" is New York City's largest park and offers a diverse range of outdoor activities. It features hiking trails, a sandy beach, and numerous sports fields. Orchard Beach, often called the "Bronx Riviera," is a popular summer destination within the park.

Diverse Neighbourhoods

The Bronx is a borough of neighbourhoods, each with its own unique character and cultural identity. Let's explore a few of them to get a taste of the Bronx's diversity.

The South Bronx

The South Bronx has a rich history and is considered the birthplace of hip-hop. The "Bronx Museum of the Arts" and the "Bronx Music Heritage Center" are essential stops here. Stroll through the streets to appreciate vibrant street art and the neighbourhood's dynamic energy.

Belmont

Belmont, often referred to as the "Little Italy of the Bronx," is renowned for its Italian culture and cuisine. "Arthur Avenue" is the neighbourhood's main street, lined with family-owned delis, bakeries, and restaurants. Savour traditional Italian dishes and shop for authentic ingredients.

City Island

"City Island" is a hidden gem that feels like a coastal New England village, despite being in the Bronx. Explore the island's marinas, seafood restaurants, and art galleries. It's a delightful escape from the urban landscape.

Embracing the Bronx's Resilience

The Bronx has faced challenges throughout its history, but it has persevered, and its sense of community and resilience is palpable. By exploring its cultural institutions, parks, and neighbourhoods, you gain a deeper appreciation for this borough's spirit and tenacity.

Exploring the Bronx: Practical Tips

- "Public Transportation": The Bronx is well-connected by subway and bus lines. The subway lines 4, 5, and 6 provide easy access to different parts of the borough.

- "Safety": While the Bronx has come a long way in terms of safety, it's essential to exercise standard urban precautions. Stick to well-lit areas and be aware of your surroundings.

- "Food": Don't miss the opportunity to savour authentic Puerto Rican, Italian, and African American cuisine in the Bronx. Explore the local eateries for a culinary adventure.

- "Events": Keep an eye on events happening in the Bronx, from community festivals to cultural celebrations. These events offer a deeper insight into the borough's culture and traditions.

Conclusion

The Bronx is more than just a borough; it's a vibrant tapestry of culture, nature, and resilience. It challenges stereotypes and invites exploration. From cultural institutions that celebrate the borough's artistic contributions to parks that offer a tranquil escape from the city's pace, the Bronx is a destination that reveals its true character when you delve beyond the headlines.

Chapter 6: Queens: A Multicultural Paradise

Queens: A Global Mosaic

Queens, often called the "World's Borough," is a multicultural paradise in the heart of New York City. With an extraordinary tapestry of cultures and a wealth of diverse neighbourhoods, Queens is a destination that offers a glimpse into the rich traditions, cuisines, and communities that make up the global mosaic of the city. In this chapter, we'll explore the vibrant cultural enclaves of Flushing, Astoria, and Jackson Heights, and uncover the unique experiences they offer.

Flushing: A Taste of Asia

Flushing is a bustling neighbourhood in Queens that's renowned for its Asian influence, making it a culinary and cultural mecca for those seeking an authentic experience.

Flushing's Chinatown

Flushing's Chinatown is a thriving community that rivals its more famous counterpart in Manhattan. It's the perfect place to savour authentic Chinese cuisine, from dim sum to hand-pulled noodles. Stroll along "Main Street" and "Roosevelt Avenue" to find a plethora of eateries, bakeries, and markets.

Queens Botanical Garden

For a tranquil escape within the vibrant neighbourhood, visit the "Queens Botanical Garden". It's a peaceful oasis featuring themed gardens, walking trails, and seasonal exhibitions. The cultural gardens, including the Chinese Scholars Garden, offer insight into the diverse backgrounds of Queens.

Queens Museum

The "Queens Museum" in Flushing is a cultural treasure that hosts a variety of exhibitions and events. Its home to the famous Panorama of the City of New York, a detailed scale model of the entire city. The museum also showcases the diverse cultures and histories of Queens.

Astoria: A Blend of Old and New

Astoria is a neighbourhood that gracefully combines the old and new, offering a taste of Greek traditions, a thriving arts scene, and a growing food culture.

Greek Influence

Astoria has a strong Greek presence, and you can find numerous Greek restaurants, cafes, and markets. Sample traditional dishes like moussaka, souvlaki, and baklava at eateries like "Taverna Kyclades" or "Zenon Taverna".

Museum of the Moving Image

The "Museum of the Moving Image" is a cultural gem for cinephiles and art enthusiasts. It features a diverse range of exhibitions, interactive displays, and screenings. The museum explores the history of film, television, and digital media.

Astoria Park

"Astoria Park" is a beautiful green space along the East River, offering stunning views of the Manhattan skyline. It's an ideal place for picnics, leisurely walks, and outdoor activities. The park also features the historic "Hell Gate Bridge", a sight to behold for engineering enthusiasts.

Jackson Heights: A Global Bazaar

Jackson Heights is a vibrant neighbourhood that stands as a testament to the diversity of Queens. It's a global bazaar that offers an array of international flavours, shopping experiences, and cultural celebrations.

Diversity of Cuisines

Jackson Heights is known for its incredible diversity of cuisines. You can enjoy authentic Indian, Nepalese, Tibetan, and Colombian dishes in the neighbourhood. Visit "Dhaulagiri Kitchen" for momos, "Arepa Lady" for Colombian arepas, and "SriPraPhai" for Thai cuisine.

Diversity of Markets

The "Jackson Heights Greenmarket" is a bustling farmers' market that features fresh produce, artisanal goods, and international treats. "Patel Brothers" is a well-known Indian grocery store where you can find spices, ingredients, and snacks from the Indian subcontinent.

Diversity of Celebrations

Jackson Heights hosts numerous cultural celebrations throughout the year. The "Queens Pride Parade" celebrates the LGBTQ+ community, while the "Diwali Mela" is a vibrant festival of lights. These events showcase the neighbourhood's inclusivity and multicultural spirit.

Queens' Multicultural Attractions

Queens offers a wide range of multicultural attractions beyond these specific neighbourhoods. Visit the "Louis Armstrong House Museum" in Corona to explore the life of the jazz legend. Explore "Gantry Plaza State Park" in Long Island City for stunning views of the Manhattan skyline. Take in the intricate architecture and serene atmosphere of the "Hindu Temple Society of North America" in Flushing.

Practical Tips for Exploring Queens

- "Public Transportation": Queens is well-connected by subway, bus, and the Long Island Rail Road (LIRR). The 7, N, W, and F subway lines provide easy access to various neighbourhoods.

- "Diverse Cuisine": Queens is a food lover's paradise. Be sure to try a variety of international dishes, from Thai and Greek to Indian and Colombian.

- "Local Celebrations": Check the calendar for cultural celebrations and events happening throughout Queens. These gatherings offer a unique opportunity to experience the borough's rich traditions and diverse cultures.

- "Cultural Institutions": Queens is home to a multitude of cultural institutions and museums. Explore these venues to gain a deeper understanding of the borough's history and heritage.

Conclusion

Queens is a microcosm of the world within the boundaries of New York City. It's a place where cultural diversity thrives, and the richness of traditions, cuisines, and celebrations knows no bounds. As you explore the neighbourhoods of Flushing, Astoria, and Jackson Heights, you'll embark on a global journey, experiencing the unique character of each cultural enclave.

Chapter 7: Staten Island's Hidden Treasures

Journey across the Harbour

Staten Island, often overshadowed by its larger and more bustling neighbours, is a hidden gem that rewards those who venture across the harbour. The "Staten Island Ferry" serves as your gateway to this less-travelled borough, offering stunning views of the Statue of Liberty and the Manhattan skyline along the way. In this chapter, we will uncover the lesser-known gems of Staten Island, from the natural beauty of the Staten Island Greenbelt to its museums and scenic waterfront views.

The Staten Island Greenbelt: Nature's Haven

"The Staten Island Greenbelt" is a sprawling oasis of nature in the midst of an urban landscape. Comprising more than 2,800 acres of protected land, it's a haven for hikers, birdwatchers, and anyone seeking an escape into the great outdoors.

Trail System

The Greenbelt offers an extensive network of trails that wind through lush forests, meadows, and wetlands. Whether you're an experienced hiker or a casual stroller, there's a trail for you. The "Blue Trail" is a popular choice, leading to the serene "Greenbelt Lake".

Greenbelt Nature Center

The "Greenbelt Nature Center" is the perfect starting point for your adventure in the Greenbelt. It provides information on the various trails and the flora and fauna you'll encounter. The center also hosts educational programs and nature exhibits.

High Rock Park

"High Rock Park" is a highlight of the Greenbelt and is home to the picturesque "Greenbelt Conservancy's High Rock Park". Here, you can explore a beautiful rock formation, woodlands, and serene ponds. The park's diverse landscape offers endless opportunities for exploration.

Staten Island Museums

Staten Island boasts several museums that offer a unique blend of culture, history, and art. These institutions provide insights into the borough's heritage and its contributions to the city.

Staten Island Museum

The "Staten Island Museum" is the borough's oldest cultural institution and is dedicated to preserving and celebrating its history and heritage. It features a range of exhibitions, from natural history and art to local artefacts.

Historic Richmond Town

"Historic Richmond Town" is a living history village that takes visitors back in time. It comprises more than 30 historic buildings from the 17th to the 19th centuries, offering a glimpse into early American life. Explore the historic streets, homes, and gardens.

Jacques Marchais Museum of Tibetan Art

The "Jacques Marchais Museum of Tibetan Art" is an unexpected treasure in Staten Island. It houses one of the most comprehensive collections of Tibetan art in the Western Hemisphere. The museum's tranquil setting and unique pieces create an immersive cultural experience.

Scenic Waterfront Views

Staten Island's waterfront offers panoramic views of the harbour and the city skyline. It's a serene place to relax, take in the sights, and appreciate the charm of the borough.

South Beach and Midland Beach

"South Beach" and "Midland Beach" are two popular waterfront destinations on Staten Island's eastern shore. They offer sandy shores, boardwalks, and a variety of recreational facilities. These beaches are perfect for a leisurely day in the sun with a view of the Verrazzano-Narrows Bridge.

Alice Austen House

The "Alice Austen House" is a historic site and a museum dedicated to the life and work of Alice Austen, a pioneering American photographer. The house, with its stunning waterfront location, offers a glimpse into the borough's past and the art of early photography.

Conference House Park

"Conference House Park" is home to the "Billop House", a historic site that hosted a critical peace conference during the American Revolutionary War. The park offers stunning waterfront views and is a tranquil spot for picnics and contemplation.

Staten Island's Best-Kept Secrets

While Staten Island may not be as widely known as its neighbouring boroughs, its hidden treasures offer unique experiences and a more relaxed pace of life. Don't forget to explore the following lesser-known gems:

- "Seguine Mansion": A grand Greek revival mansion with beautiful grounds and guided tours.

- "Postcards 9/11 Memorial": A touching memorial dedicated to Staten Island residents who perished on September 11, 2001.

- "The Garibaldi-Meucci Museum": The home of Antonio Meucci, a pioneer in the invention of the telephone, and Giuseppe Garibaldi, a legendary Italian military leader.

Practical Tips for Staten Island Exploration

- "Staten Island Ferry": The "Staten Island Ferry" offers a free and scenic 25-minute ride from Manhattan to Staten Island, running 24/7. It's the most convenient way to reach the borough.

- "Public Transportation": Staten Island has a well-connected bus system. The Staten Island Railway connects the ferry terminal to the southern part of the island.

- "Weather": Check the weather forecast before heading out, especially if you plan to explore the Staten Island Greenbelt or visit the waterfront. Dress appropriately for the season.

- "Museum Hours": Museums and cultural institutions may have varying hours of operation, so be sure to check their schedules before planning your visit.

Conclusion

Staten Island may be the city's least-visited borough, but it holds a trove of hidden treasures waiting to be explored. From the serene beauty of the Staten Island Greenbelt to the rich cultural heritage in its museums, and the scenic waterfront views that offer a different perspective of New York City, Staten Island invites you to uncover its lesser-known gems.

Chapter 8: The Art of Urban Exploration

Unveiling the Hidden City

Urban exploration, often abbreviated as "urbex," is an art form that unveils the hidden stories of the city. It's the thrill of discovering abandoned buildings, forgotten spaces, and overlooked corners of the urban landscape. Urban exploration is more than an adrenaline rush; it's a means of connecting with the past, understanding the present, and experiencing the city from a unique perspective. In this chapter, we'll dive into the art of urban exploration, focusing on safety, documenting your adventures, and the importance of responsible exploring.

The Essence of Urban Exploration

Urban exploration isn't just about sneaking into derelict buildings or venturing into off-limits zones. It's a celebration of the urban environment's complexity, layers of history, and the interplay between nature and man-made structures. Each exploration is an opportunity to uncover stories and experiences that lie hidden beneath the surface of the city.

A Sense of Adventure

Urban exploration is not for the faint of heart. It requires a sense of adventure, curiosity, and the willingness to embrace the unknown. Every exploration is a journey into the unexpected.

The Urban Landscape

Cities are ever-evolving, dynamic entities with layers of history, culture, and change. Urban explorers peel back these layers to reveal the city's secrets.

A Visual Art

Photography is a fundamental aspect of urban exploration. It's not just about documenting your journey but capturing the essence and atmosphere of the spaces you encounter.

Safety First: The Golden Rule of Urbex

Before embarking on any urban exploration, it's crucial to prioritize safety. Abandoned buildings, tunnels, and hidden spaces can be hazardous, and responsible explorers must be prepared and cautious.

Research and Planning

Thoroughly research the location you intend to explore. Understanding the building's history, layout, and potential hazards is essential. Online forums, books, and historical records can provide valuable insights.

Safety Equipment

Always carry essential safety equipment. This may include a first-aid kit, sturdy gloves, a flashlight, a respirator, and, in some cases, a hard hat and protective clothing. Safety gear can make a significant difference in an emergency.

Buddy System

Exploring with a partner is a smart choice. It provides an extra layer of safety and ensures that help is available in case of an accident. Discuss your plan and establish a communication protocol.

Respect No-Entry Signs

Resist the temptation to enter off-limits areas or trespass on private property. Not only is it illegal, but it can also lead to accidents and harm the reputation of the urban exploration community.

Documenting Your Adventures

Photography and documentation are integral to the art of urban exploration. They help preserve the history and stories of the spaces you explore.

Camera Equipment

A high-quality camera is your primary tool for documenting your journeys. Choose a camera that suits your experience level and budget. Many urban explorers prefer DSLR or mirror less cameras for their versatility.

Lighting

Carry portable lighting equipment, such as a powerful flashlight or headlamp. Proper lighting is crucial for illuminating dark spaces and capturing atmospheric shots.

Composition

Pay attention to composition and framing in your photographs. Think about the narrative you want to convey and how the elements in the frame contribute to the story.

Historical Research

Document not only the visual aspects but also the history of the locations you explore. Research the background, purpose, and significant events related to the space. This adds depth to your documentation.

Responsible Exploring

Urban exploration should be done responsibly to ensure the preservation of these hidden spaces and to maintain a positive reputation within the community.

Leave No Trace

Follow the "Leave No Trace" principle, meaning you should leave the location exactly as you found it. Avoid damaging or removing items, and refrain from leaving any trace of your presence.

Respectful Behaviour

Respect the spaces you explore and the memories they hold. Urban exploration is a form of historical preservation, and damaging or vandalizing these places is unacceptable.

Legal Considerations

Be aware of the legal implications of urban exploration in your area. Trespassing and entering restricted zones can lead to legal consequences. Understanding the laws is an important part of responsible exploring.

Preserve the Mystery

In some cases, it may be best to keep the locations you explore a secret. Sharing too much information can lead to increased foot traffic, which can harm the location or attract people with malicious intentions.

Conclusion

Urban exploration is a captivating art form that allows you to peel back the layers of the city and uncover its hidden stories. It's an adventure that requires a sense of curiosity, an appreciation for history, and a respect for the urban spaces you encounter. By prioritizing safety, documenting your journeys, and exploring responsibly, you can contribute to the preservation of these hidden treasures and share the city's secrets with others.

Chapter 9: Beyond Manhattan's Tourist Traps

Discovering Hidden Gems

Manhattan, the heart of New York City, is a treasure trove of iconic landmarks and world-famous attractions. But beyond the well-trodden paths lie lesser-known treasures that reveal the borough's hidden charms. In this chapter, we'll explore the secret speakeasies, tucked-away bookshops, and hidden gardens that offer a more intimate experience of Manhattan. We'll also provide tips on avoiding crowded tourist spots to help you enjoy a more authentic and serene visit.

Hidden Speakeasies

Manhattan is renowned for its vibrant nightlife, and some of the best experiences can be found in the city's secret speakeasies.

Please Don't Tell (PDT)

"Please Don't Tell", often referred to as PDT, is one of Manhattan's most famous secret bars. Located within the "Crif Dogs" hot dog joint on St. Mark's Place, you access the bar by entering an old-fashioned phone booth. Inside, you'll discover an intimate cocktail lounge with expertly crafted drinks.

Attaboy

"Attaboy", located in the Lower East Side, is a modern incarnation of the classic speakeasy. This bar doesn't have a traditional menu. Instead, you chat with the bartender, discuss your preferences, and they craft a bespoke cocktail just for you. It's a personalized and memorable experience.

The Back Room

Hidden behind an unassuming Lower East Side toy store, "The Back Room" is a speakeasy that offers a genuine Prohibition-era atmosphere. Sip your drinks from teacups and enjoy the nostalgia of the 1920s.

Tucked-Away Bookshops

Manhattan is a literary paradise, and hidden among its streets are charming bookshops that are a haven for book lovers.

Rizzoli Bookstore

"Rizzoli Bookstore" on Broadway is a sanctuary for bibliophiles. The elegant shop features a curated selection of books, both new and rare, in a serene and historic setting.

Albertine

"Albertine", tucked within the Cultural Services of the French Embassy, is a bookstore specializing in French and English literature. It's a place where you can explore the world through the pages of books and experience French culture in the heart of Manhattan.

The Mysterious Bookshop

For fans of mystery, crime, and detective fiction, "The Mysterious Bookshop" in Tribeca is a hidden gem. This specialty shop offers a vast collection of thrilling reads.

Secret Gardens

Amidst the concrete jungle of Manhattan, you'll find enchanting hidden gardens that provide an oasis of tranquillity.

The Garden at St. Luke in the Fields

"The Garden at St. Luke in the Fields", located in the West Village, is a peaceful escape from the city's hustle and bustle. The serene garden features a lovely fountain and benches for relaxation.

The Elevated Acre

"The Elevated Acre" in the Financial District is a rooftop park with stunning views of the harbour and the skyline. It's a tranquil spot where you can enjoy a picnic or simply soak in the beauty of the city.

The Conservatory Garden

"The Conservatory Garden" in Central Park is an immaculate space with a stunning array of flowers, fountains, and sculptures. It's divided into three distinct sections, each with its unique charm.

Avoiding Crowded Tourist Spots

To experience a quieter, more authentic Manhattan, consider these strategies for avoiding crowded tourist spots.

Off-Peak Visits

Many popular attractions are less crowded during early morning or late afternoon visits. Aim to explore these spots during off-peak hours.

Visit Local Neighbourhoods

Venture into local neighbourhoods, such as the East Village, West Village, and the Upper West Side, to enjoy authentic eateries, shops, and cultural experiences that are less frequented by tourists.

Explore Hidden Courtyards

Manhattan's hidden courtyards and mews, like Grove Court in the West Village, provide tranquil respites from the city's energy.

Cultural Events

Check out local cultural events, exhibitions, and performances. You'll often find these events to be less crowded and more authentic experiences.

Conclusion

Manhattan is a borough of endless discovery, and the gems we've explored in this chapter offer a different perspective on the city's rich tapestry. From hidden speakeasies and tucked-away bookshops to secret gardens, Manhattan's lesser-known attractions provide an intimate view of the city. By avoiding crowded tourist spots and delving into the borough's hidden charms, you'll gain a deeper appreciation of what makes Manhattan so special.

Chapter 10: The Future of Urban Exploration in New York

Pioneering Tomorrow's Discoveries

Urban exploration in New York City has always been about peeling back the layers of the past and revealing the hidden stories that make the city so captivating. As the city evolves, so too does the landscape of urban exploration. In this chapter, we'll speculate on the future of urban exploration in New York, from emerging neighbourhoods and evolving cultural scenes to the importance of preserving hidden gems while embracing change.

The Emergence of New Neighbourhoods

As the city evolves, new neighbourhoods gain prominence, offering fresh opportunities for exploration.

Long Island City

"Long Island City", in Queens, has emerged as a vibrant arts and cultural hub. The neighbourhood's waterfront parks, contemporary art galleries, and stunning skyline views have attracted a creative community. As urban explorers, you may find abandoned industrial spaces that are ripe for discovery.

Gowanus

The "Gowanus" neighbourhood in Brooklyn is undergoing significant change. Historically an industrial area, it's transforming into a hub for creative industries and tech start-ups. While this change brings new opportunities for exploration, it's essential to consider the neighbourhood's history and the preservation of its character.

The South Bronx

The South Bronx, often overlooked, is experiencing a cultural resurgence. It's becoming a hotspot for artists and creators. Exploring the area can reveal the vibrant energy and creativity that is breathing new life into the neighbourhood.

Evolving Cultural Scenes

As neighbourhoods change, so do the cultural scenes. Urban exploration in the future may involve the discovery of new art forms, performances, and experiences.

Immersive Art Installations

With the rise of immersive art experiences like "The Colour Factory" and "Meow Wolf", we can anticipate an increase in art installations that blur the lines between reality and imagination. These spaces offer a new form of artistic exploration.

Art in Public Spaces

Public art installations and murals are becoming more prevalent. The future of urban exploration may involve uncovering these temporary and evolving forms of art that enrich the urban landscape.

Underground Performances

Pop-up performances and underground events are becoming a part of the city's cultural tapestry. As an urban explorer, you might stumble upon secret concerts, theatre productions, and performance art in unexpected places.

Preserving Hidden Gems

The rapid development and transformation of the city bring about both opportunities and challenges for urban exploration. Preserving hidden gems becomes crucial.

Heritage Preservation

As new neighbourhoods emerge and old ones evolve, there must be a concerted effort to preserve the city's heritage. Abandoned buildings, historic sites, and cultural landmarks need to be protected and celebrated.

Responsible Exploration

Urban exploration should be conducted responsibly and ethically. While change is inevitable, it's important to respect the spaces we explore and to document their history. Leave no trace and educate others on the value of these hidden gems.

Community Involvement

Engaging with local communities is essential in the future of urban exploration. Building relationships with residents, artists, and preservation organizations can help ensure the preservation of hidden gems and the responsible exploration of evolving spaces.

Adaptive Reuse

The concept of adaptive reuse is gaining momentum. Abandoned industrial spaces are being repurposed into creative hubs, galleries, and communal spaces. This trend offers opportunities for urban exploration while also contributing to the preservation of these structures.

Embracing Change

The future of urban exploration in New York will be a delicate balance between preserving the past and embracing the city's evolution.

Documenting Change

Urban explorers have a unique role in documenting the changing cityscape. Capturing the "before" and "after" of neighbourhoods and structures provides valuable historical context.

Connecting with the Community

Engaging with the community and sharing your discoveries can create a positive dialogue between urban explorers and local residents. This connection can help ensure the preservation of hidden gems and cultural heritage.

Staying Informed

Keeping abreast of developments, zoning changes, and preservation efforts is vital. The future of urban exploration will depend on understanding the evolving landscape of the city.

Leaving a Legacy

As an urban explorer, consider how you can leave a positive legacy. Whether through documentation, advocacy, or responsible exploration, your impact can contribute to the ongoing story of the city.

Conclusion

The future of urban exploration in New York is a story of change, preservation, and transformation. Emerging neighbourhoods, evolving cultural scenes, and a commitment to preserving hidden gems are all integral to the narrative. As urban explorers, you have a role to play in documenting, advocating, and celebrating the past while embracing the future.

Don't miss out!

Visit the website below and you can sign up to receive emails whenever PA BOOKS publishes a new book. There's no charge and no obligation.

https://books2read.com/r/B-A-STTAB-THZPC

BOOKS 2 READ

Connecting independent readers to independent writers.

Also by PA BOOKS

Hogan's Key
Kimberly & the Five Strange Goldfishes
The Enchanted Library
The Misadventures of Pirate Pete
From Wheel To Web: 40 Remarkable Inventions
Once Upon A Sleepy Time
The Global Game - The Evolution Of Football
Strides To Success: A Beginner's Guide to Running
The ChatGPT Handbook
Climate Crossroads
1000 Everyday Life Hacks
Urban Exploration - London The Comprehensive Travel Guide
Urban Exploration - New York The Comprehensive Travel Guide
Urban Exploration - Amsterdam The Comprehensive Travel Guide
Urban Exploration - Barcelona The Comprehensive Travel Guide
Urban Exploration - Dubai The Comprehensive Travel Guide
Urban Exploration - Paris The Comprehensive Travel Guide